CALL MY
BLUFF

CALL MY BLUFF

Frank Muir
versus
Patrick Campbell

Magnum Books
Methuen Paperbacks Ltd

ACKNOWLEDGEMENTS

The popular BBC-2 game, 'Call My Bluff', was originated by Mark Goodson and Bill Todman and adapted for the U.K. by Philip Hindin

The photographs of Patrick Campbell and Frank Muir in the text are reproduced by courtesy of BBC Publications

The quotation on page 52 from the story 'The Dancing Men' by Sir Arthur Conan Doyle is reproduced by courtesy of John Murray Ltd, the publishers of *The Return of Sherlock Holmes* and by arrangement with Baskervilles Investments Ltd.

A Magnum Book

CALL MY BLUFF

0 417 01530 5

First published 1972 by Eyre Methuen Ltd
Magnum edition published 1977
Reprinted 1979

Copyright © 1972 by Frank Muir, Patrick Campbell
and Peter Moore

Magnum Books are published by Methuen Paperbacks Ltd
11 New Fetter Lane, London EC4P 4EE

Made and printed in Great Britain by
Hazell Watson & Viney Ltd, Aylesbury, Bucks

CONTENTS

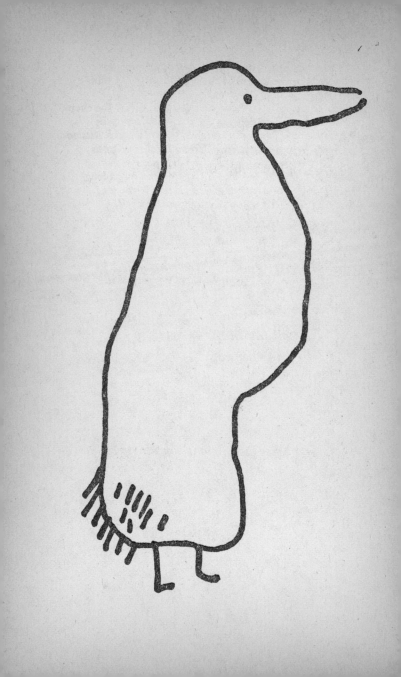

To Mr Goodson and Mr Todman of America
who were the begetters of the game of 'Call My Bluff';
To the hundreds of guests
who feared playing the game on television before the event
but ended up enjoying themselves very much;
To the compilers of the multi-volumed *Oxford English Dictionary*
who listed those obscure, weird, unlikely words
upon which the game depends;
And most of all to the BBC for keeping us for so long
in chicken sandwiches and sparkling lemonade;
This slim (but valuable) volume is dedicated.

Absolutely Everything You Need to Know
About Playing "Call My Bluff"

The television game is played by two opposing teams, each consisting of a captain (that's us) and two guests. The proceedings are controlled with considerable wit and brio by Robert Robinson.

The word in question goes up on a board and the three members of one of the teams each give a definition of what the word means. Only one of the definitions is true – the other two are downright lies. The opposing team then have to determine which is the true definition.

The only rule that matters is that the true definition really must be true. All fibs must be confined to the bluffs.

In this book version of the game we compete against each other in trying to bluff you, the reader. It works like this: the word is given at the top of the page. The one of us whose signature graces the bottom of this same page then gives three definitions, a, b and c, – one of which is the True – while the other one of us makes off-putting comments in his own fair hand on the opposite page.

The answers are given at the back of the book.

Or you can infuriate a friend by reading out the three definitions and challenging him to pick the True.

Or you can set up your own full contest and make up your own bluffs on the basis of the 100 true definitions of words given at the rear of the book.

Or you can open the book out, stand it on the floor and use it as a wicket for indoor cricket.

Good luck.

11

Part One

Here we go ~

CROCKLING

a) What a veritable feathered orchestra is provided by Dame Nature; a trilled symphony to gladden the ear of a country-dweller on a summer's morn. Over here, the cock-a-doodle-dooing of a cockerel, up to its spurs in muck. Over there, the cuckooing of a cuckoo, happily fouling another bird's nest. But what is *that* sound called, you ask? That beautiful noise made by that batch of stork-like birds, cranes? 'Why, Lord bless 'ee, sir, that noise be called "crockling". 'Tis the crockling of cranes.'

b) A 'crockling' is an over-ripe, or under-ripe, or (if there is such a thing) sideways-ripe banana, or marrow, or avocado, or even homely spud. 'Crockling' is the dealer's term for any under-privileged fruit or vegetable which, because of the lack of charm of its appearance, is invariably packed away at the bottom of the basket or punnet.

c) A 'crockling' is a lovesome thing, God wot. It is a small stone ornament, usually in the form of a bud nestling within a circle of leaves, and medieval stone-masons had the happy idea of placing them on the outside of Gothic pinnacles, or Gothic canopies, or on the apexes of Gothic arches. In a sentimental moment one might describe them as stone button-holes worn by churches.

Frank

14

Team!

Dont get nervous. And above all else — DONT LISTEN TO the DEFiniTiONs!

First game, RememBeR. Just pry into his devious mind. Would he bluff us by putting the TRUE one first? Too Bluffy. Second? Too neatly in the middle. Last?

WHY NOT!
But WHY?
STEADY

DULCARNON

a) It's not just *a* 'dulcarnon'. It's THE DULCARNON, and it'll be a trying time for all of us when it happens. THE DULCARNON – they always spoke about it like that – was the name used by the Picts – ancient Britons who were around in 400 A.D. – for Doomsday, the Day of Judgement. It's difficult for us to see what they were worrying about, in view of the fact that they were, presumably, much further away from it than we are.

b) 'Dulcarnon' sounds like a very English word – or, rather – it doesn't at all because it must surely be Scottish. But it isn't either, because it's Arabic. An Arabic adjective that means 'two-horned'. If you take a little time to work it out you will come to the inevitable conclusion that the only things with two horns are a lot of animals, very small orchestras and dilemmas, and you would be right. A 'dulcarnon' is a state of uncertainty, a dilemma.

c) A 'dulcarnon' – like a clerihew, a sonnet or a limerick – is a verse form. It has six lines which, if you can hear them from here, have rhyme endings, that go a, b, a, b, c, c, a somewhat clanky metre like a very short goods train running over points. It's named after a poem entitled 'Dulcarnon', first published in *Vanity Fair*, and written by the arthritic hand of Emily Coningsby.

Paddy

Now team, all we do is take the whole thing very calmly, making notes as we go along. Then we strike!
So here we go —

A. Rubbish.
DULCARNON can't be in Pictland — it sounds all wrong. So that leaves B. and C.

B. Its not B — if it was, the word would be spelt something like ⁊ ᚨ ᛉ ⇒

C. It can't be this one. A simple rhyming pattern like that would be much older than Victorian times.

— Oh.

17

ASKAPART

a) England during the Dark Ages was a fairly mouldy time to live in, one way and another, what with famine and invasions and Robber Barons, and no books to read – not even television. Round about the seventh century A.D. things were not improved by the activities of 'Askapart', the giant. Happily Sir Bevis rode out of Southampton at King Arthur's behest and slew Askapart and that was the end of giants with silly names.

b) An 'askapart', sometimes known as an 'evorium', and not unlike a 'reredotor', is a small chill room behind a monastery dormitory. The 'askapart' was sometimes used as a 'scriptorium' but never to store the tennis rackets. During the early seventeenth century the 'askaparts' were frequently used to house printing presses, but never, as far as is known, motor bicycles.

c) 'Askapart' is one of those adverbs you do not hear all that frequently these days. It refers to the improper drawing of a crossbow. He who draws his crossbow 'askapart' draws it 'cack-handedly', 'in a maladroit manner'. As we all know, there are five main laws of archery, concerned with the placement of hands, feet, elbows, etc. – to make sure that the beginner does not leave his arrow where it is and project himself backwards – and to disobey any one of the laws is to draw 'askapart'.

Frank

We'd better get used to it
now. The MAIN BOYISHNESS.
'Fairly mouldy time to live
in -'. Done with an engaging, but somehow Rotterish
grin. Daren't look at it for
fear of being deceived.
Draw basis of giant instead -

Bit soppy for a giant.
Oh, well ...... Bevis did
him anyway.

FROGHOOD

a) Almost absurdly obvious. There is, in fact, nothing in the least mysterious about the word 'froghood', and if frogs could speak it would seldom be off the protruberant lips of the more vainglorious among them. It simply means 'the state, or standing, of a frog' – among, naturally enough, other frogs, who would be the only other creatures to be aware of it. Was it not that well-known eighteenth-century wit Christopher Smart who rhymed:

'It's hard for any frog's digestion,
'To have his froghood called in question'?

No one knows why Christopher Smart wrote these two lines about frogs.

b) A 'froghood' was a protective cover of canvas webbing, to prevent rain getting into the touch-hole of a siege-gun. Normally, of course, a siege-gun was always kept loaded, in case any of the besieged tried to get out and had to be deterred. The first duty, therefore, of a gunner, before firing his siege-gun, was to draw back the froghood, fold it neatly and put it away in a safe place, where he knew he'd be able to find it again.

c) 'Froghood' is, as it were, the 'folk' name for a poisonous weed, which is officially known to botanists as 'the lesser hemlock'. It is believed to have been the source of the poison used by the infamous Mrs Tate of Abingdon who, at Christmas, 1808, mixed it into her mincepies, for the pleasure of passing the festival without her husband, mother, brother, father-in-law and three sisters.

Paddy

When the toad-in-the-hole is no good,
And you don't like the look of the pud,
Just summon the waiter,
And ask for a plate o',
P. Campbell-type frog-in-the-hood.

<hr>

When Lille was besieged by the Dutch,
The weather that winter was such,
That ten little Dutch souls
Got rain down their touch-holes;
I must say that war's a bit much.

<hr>

An awful old woman named Tate,
Once poisoned her family, and mate.
She baked in mincepies
'Froghood', in disguise,
Which each of the idiots ate.

QUEACH

a) A 'queach' was an early eighteenth-century cartoon. A malicious caricature calling attention to all physical peculiarities of the subject, preferably political in approach, and lightly obscene in execution. As Joseph Addison remarked to a notably unpopular and ugly M.P., 'A queach of you, sir, could not be but an improvement of the original'.

b) A 'queach' was the brain-child of a fruit farmer in California named John Josefino. His breakthrough concept was to graft a quince on to a peach – or it may have been the other way round – with the object of, primarily, making Mr Josefino a tremendous amount of money, and secondarily of providing the canning industry with a fruit-pulp of great versatility. Something went wrong.

c) Ask a stockbroker nowadays what lies at the end of his property in Surrey and he will probably reply with pride, 'There are fairways at the bottom of my garden'. 'Twas not always golf-courses. There used to be fairies at the bottom of gentlemen's gardens. Not to mention dense thickets, tangled brambles and shrubs and weeds. And that is what 'queach' means – a mini-jungle of mixed vegetation.

Frank

He does at least three
of these per game.

JOKES!

It bends the mind all sideways
to think about it.

even

'Fairways at the bottom of
my garden'.

Take it as unsaid.

No one in the world has ever
heard of a Quince-peach graft.
OR a peach-quince. OR a
queach-pence.

OR JOSEPH ADDISON.
Lies - all lies!

BONZE

a) 'Bonze' is a rather secret trade-word still used in the world of bootmaking, especially among the high-class gentlemen's bootmakers in St James. A bonze is the tracing made of the outline of a customer's foot from which, of course, the 'last' is cut. At one particular bootmakers they still have the bonzes of Lord Nelson and Disraeli, and of at least one Duke of whom it is said in the trade that he had 'a bonze like a boat'.

b) 'Bonze' is derived from the Portuguese word 'Bonzo', and is an impolite but not necessarily offensive name for a Japanese clergyman. You might wonder why the Portuguese, who live a very very long way away from the possibility of seeing even a Japanese layman, would feel the need for an impolite word for a Japanese cleric, but they do, and its 'bonze'. It's also impossible to understand why some English dogs are called Bonzo, but they are.

c) 'Bonze' was a game resembling ninepins which was prohibited-by-Statute, during the fifteenth and sixteenth centuries, on the grounds that it was knocking over too many public figures. It wasn't played in a pub or bowling alley, but out-of-doors, where there was more room for power-play bonzing: i.e. bashing hell out of ninepins painted to look like the government of the day.

Paddy

24

DISRAELI (B)

← Bonze

← Bonze

← Bonze

TAMBAGUT

a) The 'tambagut' is a bird. In size, somewhere between a turkey and a wren. By nature, affable. By instinct, bent on self-preservation. In appearance, not unlike a jumbo-sized robin. Distinguishing marks, little bristly whiskers beneath its beak, like a Guards officer. Official name, the crimson-breasted barbet of the Phillipines. Credit rating, nil.

b) It is seldom that the English language yields up its secrets so serenely as it does with the word 'tambagut'. For indeed, 'tambagut' is a species of gut used for stringing a 'tamba'. Sceptics who are dissatisfied with this explanation and wish to test it empirically need only travel to the district in and around Venezuela, call for the mandolin-shaped musical instrument known locally as a 'tamba', and examine the gut stretched thereupon. A keen eye will immediately perceive that 'tambagut' comes from an interior portion of a South American hill sheep.

c) Had you been an English milord wandering the streets of Cologne in the seventeenth century, give or take a week, you would frequently have been accosted by beggars crying 'Bitte, geben Sie mir ein Tamba, squire!' (the accent is approximate). For a tamba was a small but, to beggars, meaningful coin worth five pfennig. Thus – a any rate, that's the story – 'tambagut' came to mean 'generous', 'kind-hearted', 'not short of a penny'.

A TamBagut, on dry land?

Just possible.

Interior Portion of Hill
Sheep.

YE·ES.

'Geben sie mir ein tamBa, SQUIRE!'
Who does he think he is? 'I mean,
'WHERE does he think his BEEN?'
N'est nicht, mate?

STRAPPLE

a): It is one of the oddities of the English Law that if you are gored by a bull, nudged by a sheep or even bowled right over by a charging goat you can sue the owner of the offending animal – provided, of course, that the assault occurs on the farmer's 'strapple'. The 'strapple' is 'a path between the gate of a farmyard and the door or entrance of the farmhouse'. Lawyers favour such cases in that the limits of a strapple are quite hard to define.

b) A 'strapple', which an ignorant person might take for a lady's skirt-hanger, is in fact a special little gadget that butchers use for hanging up the more slippery raw materials of their trade. Stuff like liver, kidneys and so on that might be spoiled by the hooks that support the carcases themselves. The more jovial type of butcher has been known to say to a favourite lady customer, 'What about a nice little bit of strapple then, madam.' She should not strike him in the face.

c) A 'strapple' was a strip of Early English wool with which an Early Englishman kept his shins warm in the early morning and, in winter, for the rest of the day. It was a kind of legging or puttee that was wound round and round the leg from knee to ankle. Careless Early Englishmen, in a hurry, often wound them round too tightly, giving themselves Early English varicose veins.

Paddy

I don't know how you feel
about this definition — indeed, how
could I, apart as we unhappily
are? — but surely this piece of
land is very much the farmers'?
Which should make one even more
likely to fail in an action for
damages? But then the law –
I say nothing of close colleagues –
is an ass. So ....?

😏

Yes, but what _was_ the gadget?
How was it designed to retain
slippery giblets, one asks. However –
every butcher according to his
lights

🙁

Wool? _Wool_? Leather, surely, if
at all. Anyway it sounds a
bit effete for the peasantry to
bother about warming their bent,
hairy legs.

SUNT

a) Approach any affable joiner and cabinet-maker. Make yourself known, and bring the conversation round to 'sunt'. It is all Lombard-Street to a Clockwork Orange that he will give a small cough and recite, 'Wood that is sunt should be placed in front'. 'Sunt' is an elderly adjective used in the trade to describe wood that is perfectly matched in grain, colour, and texture.

b) A 'sunt' is a blur in printing. It is a smudged letter, caused by a number of things, including a printer who dribbles, and a chemical spot in the paper. If a whole page appears as one blur it is due to the fact that you have a very nasty sunt indeed, or your glasses have steamed up.

c) There you are, alone in the desert wastes with the fierce sun burning down, and it is lunch time. Two immediate problems spring to mind. Where to find a little shade, and what veg. to have with the roast lamb. Merciful Providence has provided the weary Bedouin with one answer to both needs – the 'sunt'. 'Sunt' is a variety of acacia beneath whose foliage a medium-sized Arab, or non-whirling Dervish, can lie, and whose pods can be ground down to make an edible mess not unlike thick pea-soup.

Frank

It's all Lombard Street to a pair of Straw Dogs, in good condition, that the affable joiner, after a small cough, will say something else.

Dribble indeed.

ALTERNATIVE DESERT MENUS

A. Bouillebaisse of Bedouin, with Steamed Sunt.

B. Curried Camel, with Assiette of Acacia

C. Fried Bread.

DESERT DESSERT

A. Derrière of Whirling Dervish, with Whipped Cream.

B. Stewed Sunt.

SPLAW

a) A 'splaw' was almost too big properly to be described as a nail, but seeing that that was what it was, that was what many people called it – that is, those that did not use the word 'splaw'. Railway workers, however, always called it a 'splaw', as they nailed railway lines with it to the wooden sleepers. After about 1860, however, when trains began to get bigger and faster and 'splaws' ceased to stand up to their work, iron-castings called 'chairs' were used instead.

b) A 'splaw' is a copper coin that was current in Scotland from about 1450 until the Union of Scotland with England in – a moment for consideration – 1603. It was slightly smaller than a bawbee, which was made of base silver, and was worth two pennies in Scottish money, or four pennies Old English. What a 'splaw' would have been in Newpence could be of concern only to those interested in such matters.

c) 'Splaw' is a splendidly expressive Northern adjective to describe a person whose boots are not under his control. It's the same thing as having two right, or left feet protruding from each ankle respectively, and both pointing in the same direction. A man who is 'splaw' walks into doors, and often falls over things like visiting-cards lying on the floor. A Northern lady, asked to waltz with a man who is 'splaw', invariably feigns deafness, idiocy or a broken leg.

Paddy

← Himself, worried.

Playing 'Bluff' from a book is much harder than on the telly because you can't see the other man's expression.

Try to imagine the man Campbell is sitting opposite you and speaking his definitions.

When delivering a TRUE definition his normal practice is to compose his features into what he imagines to be a look of baby-like innocence. In fact, he suddenly takes on the look of an ostrich which has sat in something.

The giveaway that the definition is a BLUFF is an onrush of nonchalance — a great deal of arm-waving, light laughter, whistling — and he tends to steam slightly.

MACARTNEY

a) The problem, to early nineteenth-century engineers, was how to get enough power to operate a really decent sized pile-driver. The problem, in fact, was only how to get the heavy weight up; the good Lord brought it down. The situation looked grim. Then up spake a young Scottish engineer, by name Alexander Doone Macartney, 'Eureka!' (though in his native tongue) – and he produced, for all to see, a small portable steam donkey-engine, known as a 'Macartney', which could not only be attached to pile-drivers but could be used to warp ships in and out of harbour, and even work cranes. As one satisfied customer might well have said, 'I can't imagine how I could have managed without my Macartney, the noo.'

b) There was this fellow Kit Macartney who, in 1882, landed in Perth, Australia, after having made an assisted passage from England. His passage was assisted by a judge, who objected to young Kit engaging in an affray in Liverpool which resulted in grievous bodily harm being inflicted upon a publican and, curiously, a tree. Within hours of landing in Perth young Macartney was again taken up for Assault and Battery, and during the rest of his short but active life he was arrested some nine times for the same offence. Small wonder, then, that any rumpus, hullabaloo, or noisy party in Australia is known as a 'Macartney'.

c) A 'Macartney', it would be nice to be able to state, is a beetle. But it isn't. Any reasonable man would know that a thing called a Macartney could not, in any circumstances, be a beetle. No, as the name suggests, a Macartney is a particular kind of Chinese pheasant. It has two feet, and feathers, and a fiery-red back, and it was named Macartney after the keen-eyed Englishman who first noted it, Lord Macartney – our ambassador to China in the eighteenth century.

Frank

WORKING DRAWING OF
MACARTNEY STEAM ENGINE
WORKING.

—

① Hoisting pile driver from
Hole in ground. → Pulley.

→ Rope

Hole ←

Engine
not seen.

② WARPING SHIP INTO PORT.

Ship, not seen. ←   WARP   Engine, invisible →

NEXT, PLEASE — and quick!

CHALAZION

a) A 'chalazion' is a Middle-Eastern meteorological phenomenon. It's a wind or, to be absolutely precise, a katabatic wind, a well-known scourge for people wearing wide-brimmed straw hats which are slightly too large. The katabatic, of course, doesn't blow sideways but downwards, so that the traveller, exposed to such an assault, suddenly finds that his ears are inside his hat, and he can't see a thing. This mostly happens in the valleys of the Sarakit Mountains in Asia Minor, at the time of the equinox.

b) 'Chalazion' is a purplish dye obtained from a Greek prawn found in the waters of the Ionian Sea. Unlike British prawns, which go pink when boiled, these chalazions stain the water a rich, regal purple. 'Smalls', when dipped into chalazion water, turn the same colour. For safety, and comfort, it is advisable to remove these extraordinary crustaceans first.

c) This fine old word is a gracious euphemism for what is named and called by vulgar persons 'a pimple'. It's a useful word. After all, one can scarcely tell a lady she has a pretty pimple on her nose. How much more elegant to say, 'But what a charming chalazion', even if it's impossible to guess why a true boulevardier should wish to bring up the subject at all.

Paddy

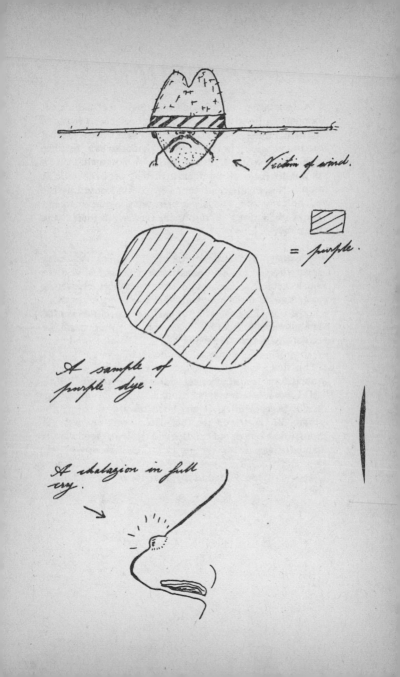

Victim of wind.

= purple.

A sample of
purple dye.

A chalazion in full
cry.

TIBBIN

a) Many a father, kind to dumb animals, well-educated, au fait with politics, has been nonplussed and made to feel inadequate by a child saying to him, 'Father, what is the name given to the topmost, that is to say, smallest tile of a roof which has been clad with Cotswold stone?' He would have avoided chagrin had he been able to reply, 'The smallest, or topmost, tile is known as the "tibbin", Arnold. The larger tiles, working downwards, are the "marstons", "bullfinches", "Welshmen", and "Jack Perrys".'

b) Consider, for a moment, the humble camel. When the caravan comes to rest beneath the date-palms, and the camel-wallahs gather round the water-hole chattering excitedly and munching sun-warmed sheeps-eyes, what has the camel been given to eat for his tiffin? He has been given 'tibbin', if his Arabian luck is in. For 'tibbin' is husks of wheat provided as camel-fodder, and very nicely it slips down too, with a drink of water.

c) A 'tibbin' is a kind of second-hand, or reconstituted, candle. That is to say, it is a candle made up of the stumps of old, used candles. In the good old days, before the advent of gas-driven weather-cocks and the horseless sausage, the bits of old candles and the waxy icicles were gouged away from candle-sticks, melted down, and re-moulded with a bit of string in the middle. 'Tibbins' were usually presented to the poor; or poor relations.

Frank

This is one of the AWFUL BITS.
He knows perfectly well it's
his turn, but he just sits
there in total silence, with
his glasses on, staring at the
desk in front of him occasionally twitching his bow tie with
his Adam's apple, and it seems
that nothing will ever happen
again. Then, some internal
disturbance seems to remind
him of his duties - and he's
AWAY! Off with the glasses
and on with this SAGACIOUS,
QUIZZICAL, OMNISCIENT,
(censored) style - "The smallest,
or topmost, tile is known as the
tiBBin, Arnold." ARNOLD!

And on & on - "Consider, for a
moment, the humble Camel. When
the Caravan comes to Rest beneath
- Ethel M. Dell at her very
worst. ON and ON and ON an

GRIMTHORPE

a) There are four kinds of 'grimthorpes', each fundamentally more unpleasant than the other. There is a 'standing grimthorpe', a 'swinging grimthorpe', a 'left-leg grimthorpe' and, finally, just before the bell, a 'right-leg grimthorpe', which often causes the grimthorpee to scream for mercy, because once the grimthorper has laid it on he can't really stop. They are, of course, all variations of the same throw at Cumberland-wrestling. There might be some value in pointing out that to the expert they are commonly known as 'hipes'.

b) Quite obviously, this word 'grimthorpe' is eponymous, being named after the *first* Baron Grimthorpe, the one who made such a hash of restoring St Alban's Cathedral. Baron Grimthorpe stuck everything he could think of on to the fabric of the fine old building, much of it on a slant, or even upside down. Hence the verb 'to grimthorpe' means to 'restore an old building with more money than taste'. It is a solemn thought that without 'grimthorping' the name of Sir John Betjeman might not have reached so wide a public.

c) 'Grimthorpe' was a strong, heavy, corded, rich-looking silk fabric, often interlined with canvas, that once was used for making ceremonial garments, such as tabards, for heralds, and chasubles for bishops. It was woven near a hamlet called Grimthorpe, in Lincolnshire. Population at last census – 2,333. Early Closing, Wednesdays.

Paddy

← A Left Leg
(As used in the
'Left Leg grimthorpe')

Old Church which
has been heavily
grimthorped (inside)

Small bishop walking in a very heavy
grimthorpe chasuble. (He has doffed his
hat because of having to lean forward)

IRPE

a) An 'irpe' is a kind of silent way of saying 'hoity-toity!' and was much used by Victorian maidens cornered by unwelcome suitors in the shrubbery. It is a toss of the head. Novelists, instead of writing, ' "Begone, sir," cried Lady Maude, tossing her head', could quite correctly have written, ' "Begone, sir," cried Lady Maude, giving an irpe.'

b) This word 'irpe' has been lying around practically unused since the marauding Danes brought it over with them around 900 A.D. I think, on a Wednesday. For all practical purposes, as far as our litter-conscious modern world is concerned, they could well have taken it back with them. It is my duty, but not my pleasure, to tell you that an 'irpe' is a long dead, unburied carcase.

c) Citizens who enjoy a wood fire blazing in their inglenook will tell you that the best 'irpe' is oak, or ash, or hornbeam, or, if a fragrant pong is desired, one of the fruit woods like cherry. One of the worst 'irpes' is spruce-fir, which is apt to spit and set fire to the cat. But any log or hunk of dead tree used to warm one's hearth and home is an 'irpe'.

Frank

Imagine what would have become of Victorian literature if all this iRping had Really gone on. I can't think, off-hand, of any examples of Victorian literature - perhaps early Agatha Christie - but if all the ladies were going to iRpe the moment they got proposititioned the whole thing would have ground to a halt in one tremendous eructation.

—

Not Wednesday. Thesday, 9.25 a.m.

—

ANOTHER JOKE!

'Spit and set fire to the cat!' Will nothing stop it? Can NOTHING be done? Is there truly no Release?

STRONGLE

a) 'Strongle' is a word from the venerable sport of wrestling – not the kind perpetrated in nylon leotards and diamanté trunks, but the more wholesome version still engaged upon, without pre-arrangement of the result, by young men in Cumberland. To 'strongle' your opponent you envelop him in a bearhug, whilst concentrating on his kidneys with whichever foot the 'strongler' may find available. The hold can only be broken by both players falling down.

b) A 'strongle' is an unpleasant little threadworm that causes disease in grouse, and on one occasion an appalling witticism, perpetrated, upon the moors above Glenfiddich, by a distressed stockbroker whose wife had just left him that very morning. 'A strongle,' he said to his beater – one of the few who hadn't already gone home in despair – 'a strongle might be amusing enough to you, but it certainly gives the bird something to grouse about.' The beater turned away and lit a short, stubby pipe. There is only one other thing of note about a strongle. Its Latin name is about two inches longer than the creature itself.

c) If beer is to be clear, not cloudy, it needs to be strongled. To 'strongle' means to strain beer and to give it a polish, although, of course, it is only the small, local brewer, whose time is not intruded upon by take-over bids and similar worries, who has the opportunity and, indeed, the patience, to 'strongle' to any effect. One of the best ways to strongle beer is to pour it through a mixture of silver sand and powdered charcoal. It makes for a heady but sometimes gritty brew.

Paddy

Hairy wrestler, after being
savagely strangled by a
powerful adversary.

Male strangle: } Female strangle: }

Small strangle: }

Medium-sized sleeping strangle: ⌇⌇⌇

Baby strangle: •   Twins: ••

Beer with polish.

GORBLIN

a) If you should find yourself with time on your hands in Egremont, Cumberland, during the month of September, do not hesitate. Buy your way into the centuries-old Egremont Fair, if only to see the centuries-old 'Gorblin Game', which seems to consist of a centuries-old local grinning through a suspended horse-collar. If the rules of the game are difficult, console yourself that you do at least know that a 'gorblin' is a Cumberland horse-collar.

b) The best time of year for 'gorblin'-spotting is in the Spring. Double-up, with one ear touching the knee-cap, and back slowly along a country hedge, peering at the lower branches. When you find a gaping beak, pointing north, you have spotted a 'gorblin'. A 'gorblin' is an unfledged bird.

c) A 'gorblin' is not at all a nice thing to happen to one, but that is life. A 'gorblin' is an error, mistake, boob, or gaffe, perpetrated because of ignorance, inattention, boredom, or being suddenly taken drunk. Whatever form it takes – clapping the first movement of a symphony, using the holy-water stoup as an ash-tray, sneezing into the sugar – one's immediate reaction is to mutter silently, 'Oh crumbs, I've done a gorblin'.

Frank

Apropos of this GORBLIN meandering, I've just remembered that Tambegut that flew in a while ago.

Remember?

But birds, even Tambeguts, don't look like that. Surely they look like this?
Un fledged, of course. You might like to fledge it yourself.

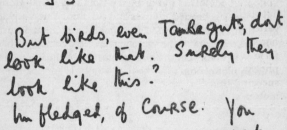

Specimen fledging, for Guidance

ERGASY

a) An 'ergasy' is, in the stilted language of pedants – and you're too slow if you get caught by one of *them* – 'any form of literary production – any piece of prose or poetry, whether written with a quill, or pen, or pencil, or a child's crayon, or a short piece of stick dipped in blood'. Thus, all the works of Shakespeare are an ergasy. And so, too, are shorter messages scrawled on walls.

b) 'Ergasy' is a wayside herb that looks like shreds of exhausted lettuce. In some parts of the country it's known as 'the catapult plant', because of the Y-shaped conformation of its leaves. It doesn't really do anything for anybody, smelling as it does, very faintly, of old furniture polish.

c) 'Ergasy' is the ancient rite of burning bedclothes, and not only bedclothes but ordinary clothes as well – things like trousers, beaded blouses and waistcoats. It's a word that first came into use at the time of the Great Plague, when the effects of the victims were ceremonially burnt by the survivors, in the hope of purifying the home, and making more room.

Paddy

Peter Moore
versus
You

Quiet, balding, country-loving, dog-patting, dictionary-eating Peter Moore now takes over from Campbell and Muir, the Old Firm, to provide your entertainment for the next section of this book.

Turn the page over and you will find on the next few pages what appear to be extracts from a number of literary works.

But – on each page, only *one* paragraph is genuine: the other two have been written by Peter Moore in the style of the original writer.

Can *you* spot the genuine paragraph? Is it A, B, or C?

(Our score is one right between us.)

from *Eric* or *Little By Little* by
FREDERIC WILLIAM FARRAR

A. With clasped hands Eric stepped forward from the ring of boys and gazed earnestly at the stern countenance of the Headmaster.

"Oh, Doctor Rowlands, thank you, thank you! By sparing us from expulsion you have saved our parents from the disgrace of our follies." Yet as he spoke he formed a wish that Vernon, his own brother, had had the manliness to come forward.

As if in answer to this unspoken thistledown of hope –

B. – a timid hand knocked at the study door and Vernon entered. With modest steps, and eyes cast down in sorrow, he approached Dr. Rowlands.

"Oh, sir, do not think too hardly of poor Eric," he said with faltering voice, "I have come to entreat for his forgiveness: to speak for him."

Though the words were of humble tone such was the boy's fervour that the hands which clasped his straw hat were white to the knuckles.

C. "I *have* just forgiven him, my little boy," said the Doctor kindly, patting his stooping head; "There he is, and he has been speaking for himself."

"Oh, Eric, I am so, so glad, I don't know what to say for joy. Oh, Eric, thank God you are not to be expelled," and Vernon went to his brother and embraced him with the deepest affection.

Doctor Rowlands watched the scene with moist eyes.

A. It was a wild, tempestuous night towards the close of October 1894. All day an equinoctial gale had raged through Baker Street, beating against our windows like some malevolent spirit bent upon invasion of our cosy sanctuary. At every gust the very house itself seemed to quake and cower before the fierce onslaught of Nature.

B. Holmes had been seated for some hours in silence, with his long, thin back curved over a chemical vessel in which he was brewing a particularly malodorous product. His head was sunk upon his breast, and he looked from my point of view like a strange, lank bird, with dull grey plumage and a black top-knot.

C. "I observe, Watson," said he suddenly, "that your barber is left-handed, plays the cornet, and walks with a limp."

I stared at him, amazed. "But how could you possibly know that?" I cried.

With twinkling eyes he reached for the old clay pipe with which he rounded off his working day.

"Elementary, my dear Watson," said he.

from the label on a bottle of
ANGOSTURA BITTERS

A. Noted originally for its therapeutic properties as a febrifuge and tonic, the bark of the Angostura, (*Galipea cuspara*), was first prepared for culinary use by Dr A. M. Mayorga in 1886, and Angostura Aromatic Bitters, (R.D. No. 228018), is still prepared from his original process.

B. As a unique and delightful flavouring Angostura Aromatic Bitters was first recognised at the International Food Exposition in Liège in 1892, and has since earned high commendation the world over. Because of its subtle and appetising aroma it is a particular favourite in the preparation of cocktails and other alcoholic beverages.

C. It also imparts an exquisite flavour to soups, salads, vegetables, gravies, fish, grapefruit, mixed cut-fruits, stewed prunes, stewed figs, preserved fruits, jellies, sherbets, water-ices, ice-cream, sauces for puddings, hard sauces, plum-pudding, mince and fruit-pies, apple-sauce and all similar desserts.

from *Petals in the Wind* by
ANN DEERING

A. He took her hand, lying so innocently in her lap. Her face was so close to him that he could feel her breath upon his cheek. "I love you, Toni . . . love you, I say!" He caught her to him swiftly, gripping her shoulders, his lips seeking hers, clinging. She was so slender and pliant, like a young sapling, he thought.

"Garth!" Would he never let her go? "Garth, my hair!"

B. "I claim you, Toni!" His arms were about her now, his lips urgent. "Garth, stop!" No, not like a young sapling – now she was like a butterfly, beating vain wings against his breast.

"Toni! Carissima!"

"No, Garth!" Was this the same ice-cold Garth she had danced with at Roundelay? Were these the same lips that had spoken so chillingly of her ambitions?

But now those lips had found hers. . . . .

C. Why was the world spinning so? What were these bright colours that flashed before her closed eyes? And why was she melting – melting like snow? Like snow – and yet strangely, as in a dream, there was fire, too.

She broke from his arms, breathless, trembling. "Have you forgotten," she faltered, "that I am engaged?"

"How exceptionally civil of you to remember me, my dear!"

At the door, hand on hip, stood Derek Waterfield.

From *All Rome and the Vatican* by
EUGENIO PUCCI, translated by SUSAN GLASSPOOL

A. It is with the stooping posture of humility that we are
commending the City of Rome to the traveller who desires
to inhale the subtle perfumes of antiquated glories or who,
to the contrary, aspires to discern the "trendy" magnifi-
cence of the Modern Era which in the Eternal City walk
hand-in-hand together, both here and there, marching in
step, suffusing in harmony the Past and the Present
without, at any times, the one suffocates the other.

B. For those who wish to enjoy the always suggestive views of Rome as it was, they must put a foot on the Esquiline, on the Gianocolo, on the Aventino to the Celio to find themselves opposite a flowering of allotments and gardens in which it is enough however to deviate for a little to re-enter into the agitated torment of the citizens' traffic that makes them lament the calm atmosphere that they have left.

C. Yet even here there is the acquisition of consolation despite the lack of repose, whether it is for him who sits at sidewalk café and imbibes the loquacious wines of Italy, or whether it is for her who saunters the shops on approval or surveys the age-old statues and fountains at which it is inconceivable to gaze without being sensible of the evocation that she is touched at the bottom.

from *The Holy Fair* by
ROBERT BURNS

A. Frae a' around guid gawsie folk,
    Owre burn an' brae are flittin,
    Frae Curchie Cross to Galvinauch,
    Wi' bawsant faces glitt'n.
    Frae caird an' cairn, frae manse an' moyse,
    Gaed monie-gilded kyvies,
    A' stoiter'd up to tak' their toise,
    Wi' Mauchline Fair their stivie.
                            Fu' daft that day.

B.   Here farmers gash, in ridin graith,
      Gaed hoddin by their cotters,
      There swankies young, in braw braid-claith,
      Are springin owre the gutters.
      The lasses, skelpit barefit, thrang,
      In silks an' scarlets glitter,
      Wi' sweet-milk cheese, in monie a whang,
      An' farls, bak'd wi' butter.
                        Fu' crump that day.

C.   Here Grandam Kyte, wi' leppin tread,
      Ha'es skilly flounces frawlin,
      An' whar's the mon sae kelp-a-head
      Tha' seeks to hish her yawlin?
      There Megan, fou wi' usqueba',
      Gies Parson Begg a slooshin,
      Baith biddin free at makin' fa'
      The Scottish Constitution.
                        Fu' blawn't that day.

NORFOLK-HOWARD

a) If you turn up *The Times* newspaper for June the 20th, 1862 you will see in the Agony Column an announcement by a Mr Joshua Bug that he had decided to change his name by deed-poll. Now, once a man named Bug decides to change his name, he doesn't change it to something similarly dreary, like Nit, or Campbell, he goes the whole hog. Mr Bug changed his name to Mr Norfolk-Howard. This so delighted the wits of the day that forever after the popular name for a bed-bug was – a Norfolk-Howard.

b) A 'Norfolk-Howard' is to a flower-pot what a nebuchadnezzar is to an Imperial Pint. Or look at it this way. It's bigger. A Norfolk-Howard is, not to beat about the bush, a large flower-pot. To be more precise, a very large flower-pot. A huge, huge, dirty-big flower-pot. Exactly the sort of flower-pot that somebody like Lady Annabel Norfolk-Howard might invent should she need a receptacle to house something like a giant Javanese azalea she had grown in her orangery. Which is exactly what happened. You can bath a dog in a Norfolk-Howard if you bung up the hole.

c) Many of the great figures of history were 'Norfolk-Howard' (I can't think of any examples at the moment, but they were). My wife and son are Norfolk-Howard, by my daughter and I are not. It is an old Sussex expression meaning – wait for it – left-handed. In Wiltshire they say you are 'Marlborough'. But in Sussex, according to the late Canon Rashleigh's *Annals of Sussex*, ever since the fourth Duke of Norfolk was so cack-handed that he had his shirts and coats buttoned the other side, if you are left-handed you are Norfolk-Howard.

Frank

Maddening device — "If
you turn up the Times
newspaper. etc." — when
he knows perfectly well
that the process would
take three weeks. And
then the Announcement
wouldn't be there at all,
unless, of Course it's TRUE,
when it would have to be
there —

The HOURS one spends
wandering around the Ruins
of his mind — bathing dogs
in Norfolk. Howards, which
can also be left-handed
people — or a bedding.

Everything gets so hopelessly
WOOLLY !

FANGO

a) A 'fango' is a ramshackle hide, a kind of cover made of leafy branches, in which the Alcaburra Indian lies in wait for his prey, such as pumas or edible antelope, with an occasional wild boar for starters. The word was brought back from the Amazon by various explorers, who, having failed by several thousands of miles to find Colonel Fawcett, felt they had to bring back something. Old gardeners on ducal estates sometimes refer to their smaller potting-sheds as 'me fango'.

b) 'Fango' is a slang word supposed to have been coined in Colchester Military Prison, round about the time of the Crimean War. None of the military prisoners, of course, had got to the Crimea, since Florence Nightingale, according to popular rumour, had ordered Lord Cardigan to cancel further reinforcements, seeing that her hands were full enough already, but the rude soldiery, incarcerated in the gaol, had found plenty of scope for ruderies in Colchester itself, with the inevitable result. Inside, the meat hash served up every day came to be called 'fango', probably from the difficulties of chewing it.

c) If you happen to be strolling around the outskirts of the Italian town of Bataglia, and one or both feet suddenly fly from under you, you can be sure, as you lie there nearly senseless, that one or both feet have slipped on a lump of 'fango'. Fango is a very special kind of mud which, if sloshed on in the form of a poultice, is alleged to ease the torments of gout. A lot of it used to be imported to Bath Spa, for the treatment of Anglo-Indian colonels, all of whom used to have gout at that time. All of them, too, used to say to the nurses, 'We'll tango after fango.' After a while the nurses ceased to listen.

Paddy.

Here are some useful spare BLUFFS
for the word FANGO:

1. A Spanish dance in which
   the body dancer is clad
   only in a fan.

2. Pet name for an earwig.

3. Old Northumbrian word for a
   digestive biscuit steeped in
   linseed oil.

4. A Burmese card-game
   played with only one card
   which is passed rapidly from
   hand to hand.

5. One of a number of FANGI.

6. An official of the Ottoman
   Empire roughly equivalent to
   a modern typewriter mechanic.

7. A poisonous berry which
   grows only in Cardiff and
   for which there is no
   known anecdote.

PIPPING

a) A 'pipping' is the half-way stage to a shot-gun wedding. It is a compulsory betrothal for a very good reason, other than mutual affection. The reason could be financial – the man has been given a double bed and cannot bear to waste half of it; social – an Earl's daughter might become engaged to a pop group's drummer in order to get invited to the best parties; or commercial – a fisherman's son and a potato-chipper's daughter.

b) Listen carefully to the word 'pipping'. Say it aloud a hundred or so times. 'Pipping'. 'Pipping'. The sound is of a tiny, fairy-like hammer tapping against a brittle, delicate surface. A goblin cobbler? An elfin convict breaking gravel? Peaseblossom, Titania's temporary typist? Almost. 'Pipping' is a noun used to describe the action of a baby chick pecking its way out of its egg.

c) 'Pipping' is a word they use in East Anglia for a short, sharp shower of rain. The essence of a 'pipping' is that it lasts long enough to require the use of an umbrella, but stops as soon as the umbrella is up. As a matter of interest, particularly to plants, a short, sharp burst from a watering-can is also a 'pipping'.

Frank

Seeing that, PROBABLY in some
ham-handed way to bring
about our down fall, he's suddenly
started doing SPARE BLUFFS,
we shall do exactly the same —
So there!

PIPPING:

① Identifying the Rank of
   army Officers, by feel,
   on a very dark night.

② An almost invisibly
   narrow border Round
   a small Arabian
   pouffe.

③ The thing a midget's
   ear does under PRESSURE.

④ Explanation of behaviour
   of German tourist, ob-
   serving Lady Godiva
   in transit.

GAVAGE

a) 'Gavage', which rhymes in part with 'all the rage', was at one time, in fact, very much all the rage, being used for keeping ladies full fore and ditto aft. It's a very tightly woven, canvas-type material, rather like webbing, which was employed as a stiffener for stays. The other romantic use that gavage is put to is in firemen's hoses which, as a result, don't often leak.

b) If we say 'savage' and, almost immediately afterwards, 'gavage', we've got an even-money chance of pronouncing both words correctly, which is more than farmers have of finding gavage in these difficult times. It's the well-known word for that part of a field which is inaccessible to the plough, like the area surrounding the trunk of a tree, or the margin beside a hedge. Now that modern farmers are tearing down trees and hedges wholesale they are losing a lot of good gavage, but don't seem to notice.

c) In hospitals all over the country nurses, with the compliance of doctors, are doing 'gavage' all the time. It rhymes, of course, with 'garage', but only in extreme cases would a garage provide accommodation for a gavage, seeing that it means the feeding of a patient by artificial means. Babies are the most constant sufferers from gavage, particularly the premature ones who are too small to defend themselves against nurses stuffing fountain-pen fillers full of milk into their ears.

Paddy

I don't think a 'Gauge' is any
of those things.   I think
that _this_ is a 'Gauge' —

(They are getting very rare)

JIXI

a) 'Look – a jixi!' was a cry frequently heard among the more ornithologically-minded Maoris as they strolled about New Zealand. In a way, a jixi is like a cow in India, except that it is a bird and it has feathers, which is more than cows can boast. The resemblance lies in the fact that a jixi, like a cow in India, is reckoned to be sacred and therefore not to be shot for the pot, or tickled, or trodden on. A jixi is the 'sacred owl of the Maoris'.

b) 'I say – jixi!' was a cry frequently heard round about three a.m. in Piccadilly, London, in the late nineteen-twenties. As any elderly ex-reveller will confirm, a 'jixi' was the popular nickname for a novel sort of taxi-cab which took to the streets, briefly, at that period. The novel part of it was not that it went sideways, or was free, or was made of cheese, but that it only had two seats (three including the driver). It was called a 'jixi' partly because it was a kind of taxi, and partly because the then Home Secretary's name was Joynson-Hicks.

c) 'Jenkins – my jixi!' was a cry frequently heard in the Highlands, round about Fort William, during the reign of Queen Victoria; or in a drawing-room – preferably facing North; or on a hillock with a clear view over Broadstairs Bay (showing the old groin). A 'jixi' was a light portable easel, once highly popular with water-colourists, and a boon to your average lady artist contemplating a quick bash at 'Stag at Bay', or 'Cox's Orange Pippin at Bay', or 'Bay at Bay'.

The only thing sacred
to Maoris is a second-row
forward called Cyril, with
fur growing down to his
eyebrows.

A Jiti was made of
cheese, and the driver
was a dry biscuit. So,
from time to time, was
Joynson-Hicks.

The old groin left
Broadstairs for Oswestry,
May 23rd, 1884, 9.15 a.m.

FEDDLE

a) A 'feddle' is a long piece of agricultural embroidery, whipped up in the autumn by, in the main, nimble-fingered Cambridgeshire agriculturists. It's a layer of willow-branches that is woven in and out along the top of a hedge. Its purpose is partly to make the hedge look neat and tidy, partly to stop it from fraying, and almost entirely to keep the feddlers out of the Barley Mow.

b) A 'feddle' is a someone, or something, who or which is pampered, is spoiled, over-cherished to the point of suffocation. It might be a wife, or an only child. It could be a hamster or a goldfish, even an aspidistra or a giant marrow. No matter if it's fish, flesh, fowl or veg. If it's doted over, it's a feddle.

c) A 'feddle' is a woollen shroud for a corpse. You'll no doubt remember that, under the Wool Act of 1670, bodies had, by law, to be buried in a woollen winding-sheet, or feddle. This, of course, was not in an attempt to revive the corpse but rather the fortunes of the flagging wool industry.

Paddy

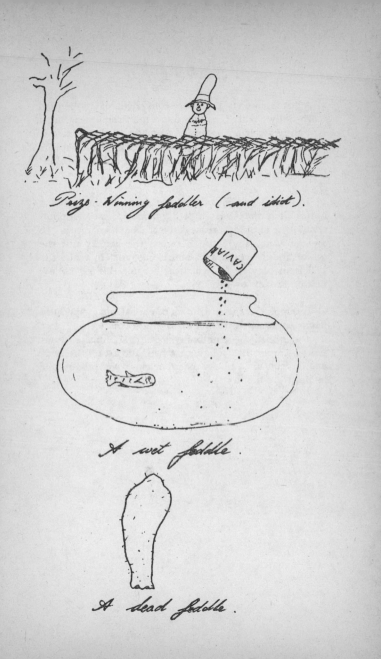

Prize-Winning fiddler (and idiot).

A wet fiddle.

A dead fiddle.

DUMPOKE

a) A 'dumpoke' is the Irish equivalent of an English 'corn-dolly', which, as you don't need reminding but I will anyway, is a human effigy made of plaited straw. The dumpoke's job is to ward off evil pagan spirits during harvesting. There are very few old 'dumpokes' left because straw rots.

b) 'Dumpoke' is a bit of cricketer's slang from the West Indies. It is the West Indians' name for the popping-crease. The popping-crease is the cricketer's name for the area of sanctuary lying between the wicket and the white line in which a batsman must remain while the ball is in play or he will hear a spine-chilling bellow behind him of 'owzatt!'

c) 'Dumpoke' is the main dish of a meal and is specially designed so as to be labour-saving to the teeth. It is a dish of boned meat or boned poultry. To make 'dumpoke', simply fillet a cow or a hen, add a capful of rice and forcemeat, and bake the lot in a low oven (about four inches from the floor).

74

← Thin.

← Bald.

← Skinny

← Untrue.

← Drivel.

← Bath water.

←——————

← Tosh.

← Meaningless.

← Hopeless.

← Dull

← Mean.

← Unconvincing,

← Worse.

← Not at all

← By No Means.

← OUT!

I'm not paying any attention to any of this because I've gone all at once, into a kind of reverie. Do you not find, in the mellow late-afternoon of life, that the mind tends, without any clear warning, to slip into - as it were - neutral, when it should be pulling strongly in, at least, third gear.

THIRD GEAR!

A Boutique on 3rd. Avenue? The saint which is older than the other two? Does anyone happen to know the right time?

STRADDLEBOB

a) 'Straddlebob' is a word of American origin, pronounced, no doubt, in the state of Wisconsin as 'straddlebahb', where he comes from. That is, a 'straddlebahb' is an inhabitant of the city of Milwaukee, which is in the state of Wisconsin. It derives from the fact that the tribe of Indians who first lived in Milwaukee had the reputation of being extremely bowlegged.

b) 'Straddlebob' was a name given by the English in the nineteenth century to an extraordinary kind of Flemish loom which instead of, as it were, looming out ordinary stuff in fact turned out an open-work fabric looking like lace. It's probable, but by no means certain, that it was called 'straddlebob' because the operator straddled a seat shaped like a saddle.

c) 'Straddlebob' is one of the curious names – there are a lot of them – given to the crane-fly, which is, of course, a two-winged fly of the genus *'tipula'*, also known as a 'Daddy Longlegs', or a 'Father Longlegs', or even in extreme cases a 'Harry Longlegs'. It's just conceivably possible that the name straddlebob comes from the insect's ability to spread its legs over, of all things, a shilling.

Paddy

If you would like a change
from pondering upon STRADDLEBOB
here are some alternative thoughts
to think upon —

① Do you realize that if
colonic irrigation had been
available at the time of
Martin Luther we might all
still be Roman Catholics?

② Do you realize that a Black
Beetle is not a beetle but
a Ladybird is?

③ That the Icelandic word for
'journalist' is 'blithermeister'?

④ That Henrik Ibsen glued a
piece of mirror inside his top
hat so that he could comb
his whiskers at the café-
table?

Hm?

77

ABLEWHACKET

a) This is a difficult word to explain so please follow me closely or I may disappear round a corner and then you will have to find your own way home. Right? Go? 'Ablewhacket' is a card game, rather like whist. It is called 'ablewhacket' because it is played by able-seamen – which explains the 'able' bit. The 'whacket' bit comes in when one of the able-seamen loses; he has to hold his hand out so that the winner can whack it. Ablewhacket.

b) Well, there you are; it's gone half-past ten and all the cider apples have been through the press, the juice run out into the vat and barrelled up ready for the next process, which is fermentation. Before putting the lights and the cat out and calling it a day, what about that stuff still lying in the bottom of the vat? The residue? Part pulp, part juice? Tell you what to do with it – call it 'ablewhacket', because farmers buy ablewhacket to enrich pig-swill, and sell it by the gallon.

c) A slight touch of the 'ablewhackets' is not a particularly valid excuse for the likes of you and me to take a day off, but it works well in the hen world. Its medical name is 'febrile gallinosis', which is no help to your average hen who has enough trouble getting her beak round 'ablewhackets', and it is a species of feverish chill. Symptoms – a general lack of interest in Life, disinclination to stand upright, and a dull look in the eye which seems to say 'I couldn't get to work on another egg if you paid me'.

Frank

Why not disappear Round
the CORNER before leaving
us with this demented
deBRis?

Artful inside Knowledge(?)
of cider pressing. WHY
does it stop at 10.30?
A.M.? P.M.? WHY <u>DIE</u> all
the time? ARE YOU?

It isn't Called 'feBRile
gallinosis', but 'Down
Behind' and its worse
and it deserves to be
Called WITABLECKET,
if anything.

LOADUM

a) 'Loadum' is a game of cards for two or more players, but not so many that you have to go out and buy another pack. The niceties of loadum are almost non-existent, so there is little point in explaining them, but if you want to win at it one thing must be firmly understood. The loser in loadum is the winner, so therefore if you want to lose your shirt try to win.

b) 'Loadum' is a word occasionally heard in places like Lincoln's Inn and the Inner Temple. It's delivered with roars of raucous laughter, or in a shocked legal undertone. A 'loadum' is an illegal agreement by a legal man to take a share of the loot received in an action as his fee. It's also known as a 'pactum de quota litis'. Put like that only the lawyers know what they're talking about. The clients find out later.

c) 'Loadum' is a disease that affects rye – the stuff used for making bread, American whiskey and for 'comin' through'. It looks like a fungus but isn't. If eaten raw, it can make you feel your last hour has come, and it often has. Thus, if in doubt, always buy overbaked crusty rye bread, rather than underbaked, or the loadum will surely get you.

Paddy

BEWARE

THE FOLLOWING CLASSIC BLUFF
TECHNIQUES, VIZ AND TO WIT:

a) He pretends it's a game
because 'Loadum' sounds a
bit like 'Ludo'. He has
also made the rules weird
to tempt you to choose it
as the most unlikely.

b) 'Loadum' sounds vaguely
Latin so a legal definition
makes sense. And a Latin
quotation gives weight to
a weak bluff.

c) He has used the old trick
of referring to something you
know to be true — in this
case that villages in France
have been sent loopy by
tainted bread.

But which definition is true??

POOGYE

a) How frequently the warm, spiced air of an Indian evening has been graced with the lambent sound of your actual 'poogye' wafting across the bungalow forecourt. Yet the 'poogye' has ever been an object of mock to those living West of Suez. The reason for this scorn probably lies in the fact that the 'poogye' is not scraped, like a violin, or hit, like a drum, or held to the lips, like a trombone, or ridden, like a harmonium. A 'poogye' is honked, being the traditional, and lovely, Indian nose-flute.

b) Like burglars, croupiers, and amorous stockbrokers, the 'poogye' sleeps during the day and becomes active at night. An average 'poogye' is, however, prettier than most average burglars, croupiers, and stockbrokers, and unlike them, tends to cause soft-hearted ladies to go 'Aaaaah, what a little darling', because a 'poogye' is a rather attractive Malayan mongoose.

c) A 'poogye' has undertones of Wilkie Collins' *Moonstone*, not to mention 'The Green Eye of the Little Yellow God'. It is a holy marble. Marble in the sense of a moggy, not in the sense of that hard stuff that Michaelangelo hacked away at. The importance of a 'poogye' to a Kurd, from Kurdestan, is not that it is round and pretty but that it represents the all-seeing eye of the prophet Kah-Ti.

Frank

To dispose of POOGYE as
quickly as possible AND
'the warm spiced air of an
Indian evening' this is what the
creature looks' like, going down
a hole & combining, for clarity,
all three definitions in its little
furry person.

TAIL ⟶
(May not fit down
hole but if nose flute
does so will it.)

Its little ⟶
furry person.

AIR

All-seeing eye of Prophet
Kah-ti

Nose flute ⟶

Hole. ⟶

PUNTY

a) 'Punty' is supposed to have originated in the Cheddar Gorge, as an antidote to or a refreshing diluent of all that cheese. It might be described as a 'souped-up' cider, in that it's distilled after it's been brewed, the distillation being about 70% proof spirit. It is then left to 'breathe' in sherry casks for three to four months, according to taste. 'Punty' is rather bad for curates and teenagers, and absolute death to teenage curates, in case any of them might have slipped into the business while the Archbishop of Canterbury wasn't looking.

b) A 'punty' is one of the many strangely-shaped, contorted, twisted, bent and – to the non-glassblower – unusable instruments used by glassblowers the world over. It's a long, for once fairly straight iron rod with a flat plate to which the bottom part of a newly-blown bottle is affixed, thus enabling the blower to shape the neck of the bottle according to his fancy, while the glass is still molten. Even people who know nothing of glassblowing can see why the glassblower doesn't put the bottom of the bottle on the palm of his hand.

c) 'Punty' is an adjective, regional to Devon and Dorset, with a meaning so natural, so obvious, so self-evident, so – as it were – exquisitely onomatopoeic that it would be sterile, futile, otiose to make further ado of its definition. However, a concession will be made to the more obtuse. It simply means 'overpleased with oneself – irritatingly cock-a-hoop – smugly on top of the world'. There are said to be as many as seven people of this type in Devon and Dorset just now.

Paddy.

As my writing tends to be rather difficult to read, I shall type this page —

##x2x(A) 'Bunty' do͟s͟t sound to pe like $ kind if cider. T̶H̶E̶x̶R̶U̶B̶B̶I̶S̶H̶x̶A̶B̶ The rubbish about curates indicates a certain desperat ion. ͟x̶ This m̶u̶s̶t̶ <u>must</u> bw a Bluff, surely §2@ ?

Class-blowing impelemnlz make 4 an easy Blu̶d̶ff because they are X̶ @ tEchnical% butsurelythe wordbuntyismore homelyawordth an a TECHnica= word§X@@()?

I̶T̶x̶I̶S̶x̶A̶L̶M̶O̶S̶T̶x̶A̶x̶R̶U̶L̶E̶x̶O̶D̶x̶T̶H̶I̶S̶x̶Q̶A̶M̶E̶
i̶t̶x̶I̶s̶x̶A̶l̶m̶o̶s̶t̶x̶a̶x̶R̶u̶l̶e̶
It   is almosta rule og this game i̶h̶
T̶H̶A̶T̶ thaq a word siad to be 'REGIonal"
turns out to be a bLUFF.   But the odd
a̶n̶d̶ one is TRUE x̶ ! tHis is meant to ve a
    helpful comment̶x̶x̶_.

Better ?

SWERK

a) The sad and depressing fact about the word 'swerk' is that, in a dark and gloomy world, it means becoming wretched and mournful. A correct use of the word in literature might be, 'Sorry, Jack old fellow, you will have to take Gwendoline mixed-bathing by yourself. I have come over swerk.'

b) In the hurly-burly of everyday life, few of us spare a thought for the problems facing brick-manufacturers. One of the problems is what to do with the baked brick-dust which accumulates inside the oven when a batch of bricks has been removed, steaming. This 'swerk', as it is called, can be raked out. But can it not be put into the service of humanity, one asks? Indeed it can. 'Swerk' can be ground into fine powder and used in the making of industrial abrasives.

c) A 'swerk' is an Irish-type secret, black, and midnight hag. Tradition hath it that it is a reincarnation of some long-dead Kilkenny harridan, and it bodes no good for any traveller who spots it. Travellers who, in the past, spotted a 'swerk', differed as to its physical appearance, particularly after they had gulped down a few jars of Liffey-water to steady the nerves, but it was generally agreed that a 'swerk' lacked charm.

Frank

Thought Processes,
(illustrated)

①

a little of Gwendoline.

②

a lot of Swenk.

③

Quite enough of the secret,
black & midnight hag.

QUILLON

a) A 'quillon' looks best on a lady who is showing some décolletage, provided, of course, that there is not so much of her on view that it diverts attention from the quillon itself. It's an ornament for the neck and upper chest – a brooch, cameo or locket that's suspended round the jugular by a ribbon, a chain or, for the really trendy, a bootlace. It's the same idea, roughly speaking, as a dog's identity disc.

b) A 'quillon' is an oddly shaped skittle or ninepin, for bowling a ball at, that doesn't look like a wooden bottle, but more like a wooden hour-glass with a pinched-in waist. Bowling at quillons was originally a Norman-French pastime. The Dauphin, having lost his nerve altogether, is actually alleged to have had a go at it *during* the Battle of Agincourt.

c) A 'quillon' is one of the cross-guards on the hilt of a sword, the stick-out piece on each side that forms a cross with the sword itself. If you were in a fight to the death with someone it prevented him sliding his sword up yours and lopping off your thumb. It also stopped the sword falling straight through the scabbarb and puncturing your own foot.

Paddy.

All three of these definitions
are so unlikely that there is
no comment which I wish to
make. Please feel free to
use this sheet of paper for
drawing upon; or folding and
shoving under the leg of a
wobbly mother-in-law; or as
the raw material for manufacturing
all-white confetti for the wedding
of a loved one.

HICKBOO

a) A 'hickboo' is a form of silencer that Singalese mothers fit to their babies. It is a short, thickish stick that serves as a dummy, gag, and toothing-stick. Kind Singalese mummies cut their 'hickboos' from sugar-bamboo, which transforms them into lollipops.

b) A 'hickboo', in the language of the United States of America, was what is now called a 'non-event'. Non-events, which take place frequently in the modern world, are those events which, overpuffed in advance by the Press, Radio, and T.V., prove a dreary anti-climax when they actually happen. Typical 'hickboos' include the Catering Trade and Convenience Food Equipment Manufacturers Beauty Queen Competition, and the Honours List.

c) Here is a word of nostalgic memory to all those readers who recall the zeppelin raids of World War One. As the ominous silver cigar appeared in the sky, or a squadron of Gothas was sighted, loud cries of 'Hickboo, you chaps' were heard in Royal Flying Corps messes, and up went the Sopwith Pups, S.E.2's, and similar frail aircraft, in hot pursuit. 'Hickboo', as a slang word for an air-raid, did not survive the first World War.

Frank

Some Helpful Jottings.

a Kind
Singalese
Mummy.

Singalese
Silencer

British
Non-Event.

German
Sausage.

N.B. All Plans are drawn to scale.

QUOILER

a) A 'quoiler' is an artfully arranged lock of hair that's worn on the forehead, that kind of inverted cow's lick that is known as a 'kiss curl'. Historically speaking, there seems little doubt that the two most famous quoilers were those worn by Napoleon Bonaparte and Benjamin Disraeli, curls which were presumably teased or otherwise handled by Josephine and Mrs Disraeli respectfully.

b) A 'quoiler' is the same sort of article as a woman's shoulder-strap – those vital bands that support so much – except that this one is worn by a cart horse. It's a fairly wide leather strap that the cart horse wears not over its shoulders but round the lower part of its rump. By leaning backwards against its 'quoiler' the horse can put the cart into reverse.

c) A 'quoiler' is a stiff reproach or rebuke, known among the less imaginative sections of the Armed Forces as a 'rocket'. Uncouth persons like sergeant majors are apt to bawl 'quoilers' at the tops of their voices, but in polite society a 'quoiler' is usually prefaced by the remark, 'I know you won't mind me being perfectly frank –'.

Paddy

If, like me, you don't really care if a QVOILER is a brassiere for a horse's bottom, then lets play the Initial game instead. Complete the list below with suitable words beginning with the letter 'c'.

Should take you 1 min. (or less).

C.

JEWEL OR MINERAL		PART OF BODY	
TOWN		COLOUR	
NOVELIST		FOOD	
ANIMAL		RIVER	
PLANT		BOOK TITLE	
ARTIST		PART OF CAR	
POP SINGER		OATH	

ALALA

a) 'Alala' is probably the oldest battle-cry ever to have been cried in the Western World. It might have been cried in the Eastern world, too – most things, like printing, gunpowder, and oysters, started in the inscrutable East – but if 'Alala' was cried in the East it was merely an interesting coincidence. 'Alala' was the battle-cry of Ancient Greek soldiers (soldiers of Ancient Greece, that is. Some of them were quite young).

b) An 'alala' is the bedouin equivalent of a car-park. It is an area, usually near an oasis, where camels may safely graze. A tip-top, grade A 'alala' provides shade, and a little light herbage for the ships-of-the-desert to munch, before the long haul to Alexandria and a cold beer. During a recent difference of opinion in the desert, enemy troops sprayed the 'alala' with sodium chlorate which rendered them not-worth-stopping-at-able.

c) Take a hake. Transfer it to Australian waters. Treble its size. And you have – roughly – an 'alala'. This delicious fish is practically tasteless, besides being ugly, and it was very clever of it to allow itself to be caught by aborigines with a spear, and baked in leaves and herbs, so that the result was not only edible but gave the 'alala' a reputation for being a rare delight for the epicure.

Frank

THREE HOUR CROSSWORD

1	2	3	4	5
2	2	3	3	5
3	3	1	4	6

ACROSS: 1. A battlecry
2. Bedouin Car-park
3. Australian Hake

DOWN: 1. Stand at — ?
2. — ia and Doris
3. Takin' me —
4. — where, not here.
5. — Wharf.

ANSWER:

(Thank You)

—

¹A	²L	³A	⁴L	⁵A
²A	²L	³A	³L	⁶A
³A	³L	¹A	⁴L	⁷A

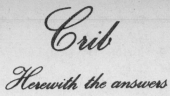

Crib

Herewith the answers

One Hundred True Definitions

Hand-picked

from the 13-Vol Oxford English Dictionary

and abridged

for those who wish to play their own

games of 'Bluff'

BEARLEAP	A Tudor housewife's large shopping-basket
OGHAM	A primitive Gaelic alphabet
BUNGIEBIRD	Rude nickname for a Franciscan monk
ACCIPITER	A bandage wound round the nose
HAMFARE	A marital difference of opinion
GUGGLET	An Indian pot of unglazed clay
MUCKLUCK	An Eskimo's boot made from sealskin
WLONK	Anglo-Saxon adjective meaning 'haughty'
SHERRYVALLIES	Velvet overalls for eighteenth-century gentlemen
PIFFER	Soldier in Punjab Irregular Frontier Force

MUMBUDGET	Game played by sixteenth-century children
YAKALO	Animal that's half yak, half buffalo
WAPPENSHAW	Open-air rifle meeting for volunteers
TOGATE	Wearing, or dressed in, a toga
SLUNKER	An elderly and unwanted female sturgeon
BULGER	A late nineteenth-century golf-club
BOMBUS	A medical synonym for the collywobbles
BRAXY	Splenetic apoplexy in sheep
PRIMSTAFF	Wooden almanac of Icelandic origin
QUIDDANY	Jam or jelly made from quinces
CARCEL	Oil lamp that works by clockwork
WOODOO	A minor ablution performed by Mohammedans
SPRAINTS	The droppings of an otter
ERIFF	A two-year-old canary
BULLARY	A collection of Papal Bulls
LOOMERY	A breeding-place for guillemots
SNOACH	Verb – to breathe through the nose
BIBBLES	Geological strata containing pockets of water
WOMBLING	Adverb – with belly to the ground
SOOSY	A rich variety of Eastern silk
BILLYBOY	A boat used on the River Humber
VESPILLON	A bearer of corpses for burial
LINTWORM	A brooch shaped like a dragon
FRANTLING	The mating call of a peacock
TUMBESTER	A lady-acrobat
QUEASOM	Verb – to stifle, smother, or suffocate
SLIMSKIN	American slang for an old sea-elephant

PULLICATE	An Eastern handkerchief of coloured yarn
ZURF	An Arabian holder for a coffee-cup
AMMA	An Ancient-Greek cummerbund
HAKER	A fisherman who fishes for hake
ROBERDAVY	A strong, red, Elizabethan wine
JERQUE	Verb – to search a ship for contraband
BARGARET	A rustic open-air song-and-dance
BANDOLINE	A hair-dressing made from quinces
BOONING	The repair and maintenance of roads
GARGAREON	A medical term for the uvula
JARGOON	An inferior variety of zircon
GAFFLE	The lever for cocking a crossbow
WINX	Verb – to bray like a donkey
BUFFUM	A regional name for linseed-oil
JACKSHAY	A large tin billy-can
GANSEL	A garlic sauce to accompany roast-goose
TIVER	A red dye for marking sheep
AMBURY	A disease affecting cattle and turnips
MERROW	An Irish mermaid
LINGTOW	A rope for hauling contraband ashore
PUTCHOCK	Indian plant used for making joss-sticks
WAYZGOOSE	A recreational outing for printers
BUMBOLO	A glass flask for sublimating camphor
BUCCINATOR	A flat muscle in the cheek
GROPSING	A dialect word for twilight
CARPHOLOGY	A neurotic picking at the bedclothes
HARPRESS	A lady harpist
SPROAT	A fishing-fly invented by Mr Sproat

POLLIWOG	A dialect name for the tadpole
FATTRELS	The ends of a ribbon
ODA	A room in an harem
ANABAS	The tree-climbing perch of Madras
JIRBLE	Verb – to pour out drink unsteadily
ROCAMBOLE	A non-Welsh variety of leek
ECCALEOBION	A primitive incubator for hatching eggs
PUCKET	A group or assembly of caterpillars
SHOOFLY	An American emergency railway-siding
STRANGULLION	A disease in horses resembling quinsy
WHEWER	A female widgeon
CHERMANY	An unofficial variety of American baseball
SHOYHOY	A boy hired to scare birds
TERP	A prehistoric burial-mound in Holland
SURPOOSE	The lid of a silver vessel
LORDSWIKE	A dishonest serf or varlet
POTLATCH	A tribal feast of North American Indians
FADDING	An old Irish square-dance
TROOLIE	A hat made from palm-leaves
CANNET	An heraldic duck without beak or feet
JORRAM	A Gaelic fisherman's mournful boating-song
CACHESPULE	An antique name for Tennis
BARGHAM	A collar for a cart-horse
FLUMMADIDDLE	An edible mash of American origin
BLOBBING	A method of fishing for eels

ENGASTRIMYTH	A classy name for a ventriloquist
MINCHERY	A dwelling-place for nuns
MOLOCKER	An old, but renovated, top-hat
MOLLIE	A mid-ocean meeting between whalers
CLAGGUM	A slang word for treacle-toffee
NOPALERY	A garden for breeding cochineal-insects
MOREPORK	An owl-like Antipodean bird
WENTLETRAP	A rare and beautiful Chinese sea-shell
EGBO	An African Mafia-type secret society
COMSTOCKER	He who is affronted by nudity

Frank Muir & Denis Norden

THE 'MY WORD!' STORIES

Probably the most popular radio programme in the world, 'My Word!' has countless fans in more than thirty-five countries. Its highlights are the outrageously funny spoof explanations of well-known sayings concocted by Frank Muir and Denis Norden, which have had listeners roaring with laughter for twenty years. Here is a collection of the best of their tall stories.

'A feast of fun from two very funny persons'
—*Evening News*

Osbert Lancaster

THE LITTLEHAMPTON BEQUEST

Drayneflete Abbey—ancestral home of the Earls of Littlehampton—is famed worldwise for its magnificent collection of pictures and works of art, assembled over many generations by one of England's leading families. Until recently very few had the privilege of viewing this great collection, but the present Earl has now most generously bequeathed it to the National Portrait Gallery (in lieu of death duties). Moreover, because shortage of space in the Gallery prevents display at present, he has commissioned Osbert Lancaster to prepare this fully illustrated volume which not only reproduces the works of art—from Holbein to Hockney—but also records the achievements and aristocratic personalities of the long line of Littlehamptons.

'A marvellous book, witty and endlessly entertaining'
—*Guardian*

Thelwell

THREE SHEETS IN THE WIND

Arriving on a summer week-end at any stretch of water without one's own craft behind the car or swaying proudly at its moorings is like attending a dance with a broken leg—not to mention the damage to one's social status. Unable to bear being a second-class citizen any longer, Thelwell purchased his own boat and launched himself into unknown waters. But he found that learning to sail can be hazardous, and learning to speak a whole new technical language can be, to say the least, traumatic. So, ever mindful of the need to help his fellow men, he has produced this indispensable manual of instruction for sailors everywhere.

TOP DOG

As every experienced dog-owner knows, man's best friend is a complex bundle of appetites, instincts and winsome wiles. Few first-time pet-owners will realise, however, just what a responsibility they are taking on. So Thelwell has kindly provided them with this invaluable handbook full of advice on choosing, training, feeding, exercising and caring for our four-legged friends. It also emphasises the importance of protecting one's own interests—not to mention those of one's neighbours—for an ill-trained hound will soon develop a healthy disrespect for law and order. Here is a superb collection designed to give every dog-owner a new leash on life in the canine world.

W. C. Sellar & R. J. Yeatman

GARDEN RUBBISH

Messrs Sellar and Yeatman have provided a unique gardening guide. It includes, naturally, a scholarly account of the somewhat hazy history of horticulture, together with timely advice on such absorbing topics as the transmigration of soils, manurial rites and bastard-trenching, offered with just a few cutting remarks. This handbook may be commended to all lovers and haters of gardens, and to those who remain neutral it will afford many a provoking thought.

HORSE NONSENSE

Messrs Sellar and Yeatman now turn their enquiring pens to the subject of horses—and the people who ride, hunt and punt on them. Non-riders will find *Horse Nonsense* indispensable to their understanding of the topic: and riders will discover a lot of astonishing things about the Noble Animal which may have heretofore escaped them.

Jilly Cooper

SUPER MEN AND SUPER WOMEN
Her brilliantly funny guide to the sexes

Whatever their grading, Super Man or Slob, Super Woman or Slut, Jilly submits them all to remorseless scrutiny. In public and private, home, office or bed, none escapes her beady eye—from guardsmen to gigolos, debs to divorcees, stockbrokers to sex fiends, tarts to Tory ladies.

WORK AND WEDLOCK

Jilly Cooper's shrewd and hilarious guide to survival at the office and in marriage

Whether your particular enemy is the Office Boss or the Office Bully, the Little Home-Breaker or the Office Crone, Jilly's outrageously funny guide to the hazards of working life is a must for you. And when she turns to the Home Front, spouses and prospective spouses would be unwise to neglect her tactical briefings. Bed, Money, In-Laws, Affairs—you name it, Jilly puts her finger on it.

More top humour available in Magnum Books